pen and ink
DRAWING

by Jonathan Stephenson

ISBN 1 871517 10 9

Osmiroid Creative Leisure Series

About the Author

Jonathan Stephenson is a writer, a painter, an art historian and a lecturer. He is also a specialist artists colourman with a deep knowledge of the relationship between artists' materials and their techniques.

Jonathan Stephenson's accumulated experience covers the fields of fine art, illustration, graphic art and design. He has been working with pen and ink for many years and has an expert and varied knowledge of that medium. He has written books on *THE MATERIALS AND TECHNIQUES OF PAINTING* and on *GRAPHIC DESIGN MATERIALS AND EQUIPMENT*. He is also known for his magazine articles and regularly contributes to publications such as The Artists & Illustrators Magazine and The Artist.

The Osmiroid Pen and Ink Drawing Kit provides everything you need to start creating exciting pen and ink drawings. As your interest and skill in the art of pen and ink drawing grows, you may wish to purchase other materials to develop some of the further ideas outlined in this book as well as your own particular interests.

CONTENTS

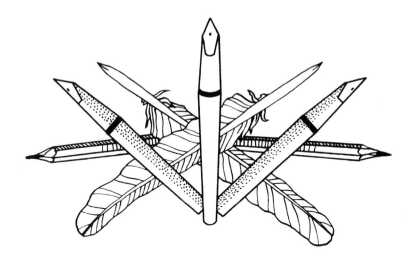

INTRODUCTION

The History of The Pen

Pens may have been in use since ancient Egyptian times. At first, they were made of reeds cut at an angle and trimmed to a broad stiff point. A reed pen makes a mark like a calligraphy pen, though it is inclined to be a little rough as its point is crude and inflexible.

The quill pen made from a bird's wing feather is first mentioned in the 7th century A.D., but it seems likely that they were in use long before that. Pens get their names from quills as the word originally simply meant 'a feather'. The point of a quill is cut in much the same way as a reed, but a small slit is introduced in order to help the ink flow. A much smaller point is possible with a quill pen and since the tip is flexible, a much greater variety of movement can be accommodated as it writes or draws. Unfortunately though, the point wears down very quickly and a quill has to be recut frequently using a pen knife. Because of this, attempts have been made from an early date to replace the quill with something more durable.

The obvious solution was to make pens out of metal, but the performance of a quill is difficult to match and it was a long time before this was successfully achieved. James Perry, Osmiroid's founder, took out a Letters Patent for the steel nib in 1830. A bronze pen was found amongst the ruins of Pompeii and metal pens were being forged by hand from the Middle Ages onwards, but these appear to have had little impact on the use of the quill. At the beginning of the 19th century, an attempt was made to replace quill pens with nibs made with tortoise shell and horn sheathed in gold or tipped with diamonds and rubies. However, only a few years later, machine made metal nibs were introduced and from the early 1830's onwards, their use became widespread.

Metal pen nibs are made from a special quality of steel and are designed so as to give good ink delivery and the maximum amount of flexibility. These features are essential for drawing nibs which must work smoothly in all directions, whilst responding sympathetically to small movements of the hand. Nowadays metal sketching nibs have reached a state of near perfection and they perform very like the original quills. In recent times, they have been combined with the principles of the fountain pen which was first introduced at the end of the 19th century. By modifying the design the Osmiroid Pen Company made it possible to use some fountain pens with India ink. Drawing pens of this type retain the essential features needed for traditional pen and ink drawing, yet they offer much greater convenience to the artist.

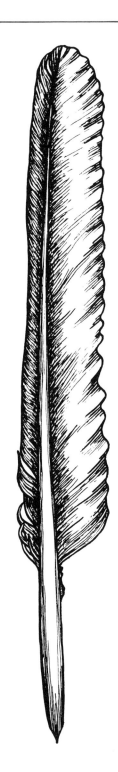

The Pen as a Drawing Instrument

The quill pen began to establish itself as an important drawing instrument during the 12th century. It is better suited to drawing than the reed pen, since its smaller and more flexible point can make a wide variety of marks and is capable of much finer detail. Reed pens may be used for drawing, but compared to quill pens, their range is quite limited. The modern equivalent of the quill and the reed are the sketching pen and the calligraphy pen. The use of both is demonstrated in this book.

At the beginning of the Renaissance, pen and ink drawing probably formed part of every artist's training, but drawing as a means of artistic expression was not yet fully developed. That began to happen under the influence of Leonardo da Vinci, Raphael and Michelangelo. All were capable of producing masterpieces in pen and ink and their drawings are still greatly admired. Michelangelo in particular took drawing seriously, and is said to have destroyed many of his poorer efforts. He also produced some presentation drawings which may have been quite carefully planned. It is from this background that formal pen and ink drawing has subsequently developed so that it now stands on its own as a medium and is no longer used exclusively for sketching or for preliminary drawings. It is this type of pen drawing that is considered in this book.

The great artists of the Renaissance used pen and ink out of necessity as graphite pencils did not then exist. Since then, many artists have chosen to use the medium for its particular qualities of expression. The pen is a much more versatile drawing instrument than might at first be supposed and it responds uniquely to each individual. Because of this, many different styles are possible and the medium of pen and ink is capable of almost endless variation. This book sets out to demonstrate the basic techniques. None are difficult to master and all are open to individual interpretation. Further inspiration might be gathered from investigating and studying the pen drawings of artists such as David Hockney, Picasso, Aubrey Beardsley, Van Gogh, Rembrandt, Albrecht Durer and Botticelli, as well as those already mentioned: Leonardo da Vinci, Raphael and Michelangelo.

Types of Pen

The simplest form of pen is known as a dip pen. These follow the basic design of the quill and the reed and consist only of a nib slotted into a pen holder. Such a pen is loaded with ink by dipping it into it, hence the name dip pen. They carry as much ink as will cling to the back of the nib, this amount increases when they are fitted with a reservoir. Osmiroid dip pens have a reservoir which is independent of the nib and so can be adjusted to optimise ink delivery to the nib. For drawing purposes a dip pen only works well when it contains a modest amount of ink, not too much and not too little, which increases the frequency with which it must be dipped into the ink. Any excess ink is removed from the nib by stroking it against the ink bottle.

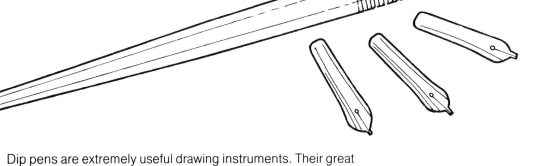

Dip pens are extremely useful drawing instruments. Their great advantage is their simplicity, since there is no mechanism to clog and replacement nibs are cheap, any kind of ink may be used in a dip pen, even paint can be used. So far as pen drawing is concerned, this is extremely important, as the principal ink that is employed is India ink. This dense black ink is quite unlike writing ink and it clogs pens easily. As a dip pen is easy to clean and has no mechanism to clog, it gives a relatively trouble-free performance with India ink.

Fountain pens are much more convenient to use since they carry a large supply of ink either in a special reservoir or in a cartridge inside the barrel of the pen. This means that they work for a much longer period of time between fillings. It also means that they can be used anytime, anywhere, without having to set up a special drawing area in which the ink and pens and paper are all laid out carefully for clean and efficient working. Fountain pens are clean and efficient anyway and are ready to use as soon as the cap is removed. What is more, they have an ink feed system which delivers a regular supply of ink to the back of the nib. This means the flow of ink through the nib is constant and the amount delivered to the paper is controlled entirely by the actions of the artist.

Osmiroid India ink fountain pens draw smoothly if they are kept clean and respond as well as any pen to the movements of the hand. These pens are designed so that the ink feed can be removed for cleaning. Ordinary fountain pens will function best if regularly flushed through with tap water. The secret of good pen drawing is absolute control over the nib and a wide choice of different nibs will enhance the range of styles available to the artist. In addition to sketch nibs, India ink fountain pens may also be fitted with calligraphy nib units. These may be employed for drawing too, and in certain styles of pen drawing they are very attractive.

One other type of pen ought to be mentioned as an instrument for pen and ink drawing; that is the technical pen. These pens are intended for draughtsmen, but they are popular with designers and some artists. Essentially they are a type of fountain pen, but instead of the conventional nib, they deliver ink down a thin tube. This allows them to produce a very even line and very precise dots. These can be useful in certain styles of pen and ink drawing, but more often the evenness of their mark is a disadvantage since it lacks the expression and energy that is so typical of conventional pen drawing. Compared to dip pens and fountain pens, they are expensive items.

Choice of Paper

Pen and ink drawings are usually undertaken on paper, though they are occasionally done on card. White paper or card is the most popular since it contrasts strongly with black ink, but there is no reason why coloured papers or decorative papers should not also be used.

There are numerous types of paper to choose from but not all of them perform well with pen and ink. Very rough papers, soft papers and lightweight papers generally do not. However there is no hard and fast rule, some papers will work well with certain pens and inks, but not with others. Even the best papers do not give good results if pens are incorrectly used. As a precaution it is always advisable to test a sample of the chosen paper with the pen and ink that are to be employed before work begins. If the nib snags, or the ink spreads, then that combination of materials is not suitable. The following types of paper and board may all be considered for pen drawing.

Cartridge paper is standard drawing paper. It is white or off white with a fairly smooth surface. Its quality varies considerably and the performance that can be expected varies with it. Usually, heavier, thicker cartridge paper works best.

Bristol Board is lightweight cardboard made from sheets of paper bonded together. It is sturdy without being stiff and makes an excellent base for pen drawing. Its surface is extremely smooth and a pen will glide across it very easily with very little risk of snagging. Bristol Board is whiter than most white papers and sets off black ink very well.

Watercolour papers may also be used as drawing papers. This is especially desirable where ink washes or watercolour are to be added over the drawing. The smooth, 'Hot Pressed' watercolour papers are best for drawing, but most 'Not surfaced' watercolour papers are also acceptable. Pen and ink will work on some rough surfaced watercolour papers but the results vary.

Some decorative papers give good backgrounds for pen and ink. They are seldom intended for this purpose however and must be tested before use. Soft colours and subdued patterns work best as they do not dominate the drawing, yet they may add significantly to its appearance. Decorative papers can be chosen carefully to reflect the subject matter of the drawing or alternatively, the style of drawing can be modified so that it relates to the paper. There are many decorative papers to choose from, but examples that might be considered are coloured imitation parchment such as is used for calligraphy, pale marbled papers, printed wrapping papers and decorative oriental papers.

Illustration board is strong card faced with good quality paper that is intended for pen and ink drawing.

A few words also need to be included on the subject of permanence. A pen drawing will only last as long as the paper it is on and only the very best quality papers last for a long time. If permanence is a consideration, then acid free papers which are described as 'all rag', '100% cotton' or as 'wood-free' should be selected. All artists papers should be of this quality, but regretably that is not always so. Some of the papers and boards listed above may not be durable in the long term, but that does not necessarily make them unsuitable in all circumstances.

Other Materials

As well as pen and paper, several other items may be needed for pen and ink drawing. Ink is obviously required. As has already been stated, India ink is the best for drawing purposes. This is a black pigmented ink containing shellac which is lightfast and usually waterproof when dry. Other inks may not possess these qualities and cannot be relied upon to the same extent, but they are still employed in order to bring colour and variety into pen drawings. Osmiroid coloured calligraphy inks are of an acceptable standard for pen drawing, but other coloured inks should be assessed carefully to see if they are fit for the intended purpose. In some applications it may be preferable to use watercolour diluted to the consistency of ink and applied with a dip pen.

The type of pen drawing considered in this book is a controlled art form which frequently makes use of a preliminary lay-in in pencil. This may also involve a carefully constructed design and it follows that an assortment of general drawing equipment may be needed to support pen and ink.

Any pencil will do for preliminary drawing so long as it is used lightly. A soft pencil produces a dark mark and gives a good indication of what the finished drawing will look like. Some artists prefer hard pencils as their faint lines are less of a distraction during inking in. They are also easily lost beneath the pen marks and may not need to be erased. If pressed too firmly, pencils make marks which may be difficult to remove completely. Hard pencils may also score the paper surface. Neither of these things are helpful in pen drawing.

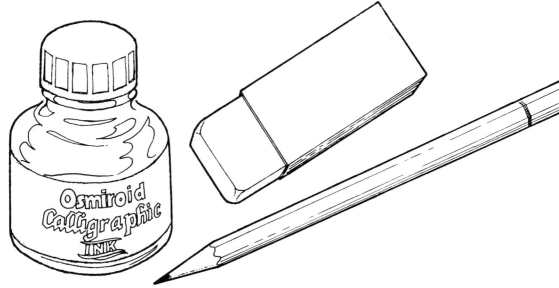

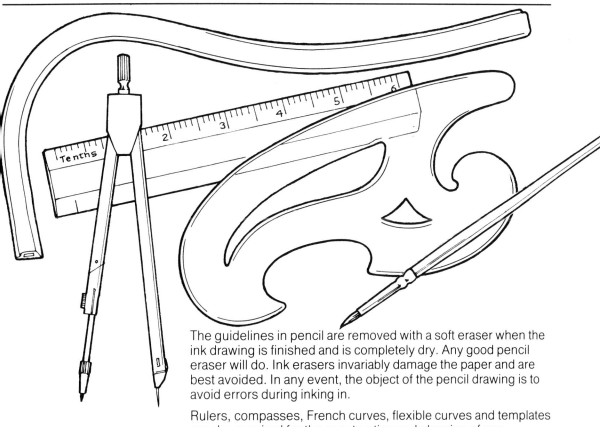

The guidelines in pencil are removed with a soft eraser when the ink drawing is finished and is completely dry. Any good pencil eraser will do. Ink erasers invariably damage the paper and are best avoided. In any event, the object of the pencil drawing is to avoid errors during inking in.

Rulers, compasses, French curves, flexible curves and templates may be required for the construction and planning of pen drawings. Preferably these should be used with pencil to create guide lines that the pen can follow as sketching pens rarely work well against an edge. If drawing pens are used against rulers or templates, they should be turned upsidedown so that the bevel lifts their edge clear of the paper. This prevents ink running underneath the edge and ensures a neat line. The straighter the line or the broader the curve, the more likely it is that a pen can follow it, but the only pens that guarantee good results when used with drawing aids are technical pens. Fortunately this is seldom a problem as perfect lines are rarely needed in pen drawings. In fact, a little irregularity in the inking in usually makes the drawing more attractive.

When ink washes or watercolours are used with pen drawings, brushes are also required. Ordinary watercolour brushes are used and one good sized brush with a fine point may be all that is required. Sable brushes are best, but they are expensive. Squirrel hair or synthetic hair make acceptable alternatives. If India ink is employed, the brush must be cleaned thoroughly in water immediately after use, otherwise the brush may be damaged beyond repair.

Basic Marks

All a pen does is deliver ink onto paper; it either makes a mark or it does not, so the artist must vary the shape and the size of the mark and must combine marks in different ways in order to create different visual effects. The only other device that can be exploited is the contrast between those marks and the paper which surrounds them.

The marks are varied by altering the position of the pen and by changing the way in which it is moved as the marks are made. They are combined by placing different marks adjacent to each other or by laying them over the top of each other. The denser the concentration of marks, the less the paper is seen; the smaller and more separate the marks, the more it is visible. Out of this apparently narrow set of principles, a surprisingly large range of effects can be extracted. If different sizes and shapes of pen are used as well, the possibilities are increased still further. Becoming familiar with the basic marks that a pen can make and investigating how they may be combined should be the starting point for any artist wanting to master pen and ink drawing.

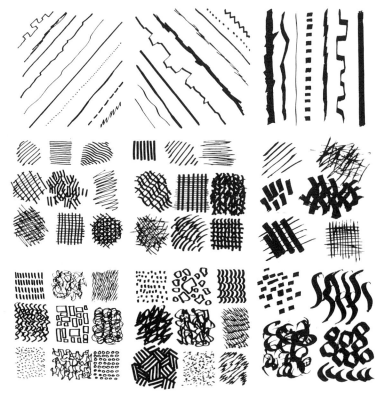

This illustration shows a selection of basic marks achieved using 3 different pens. The column on the left was drawn with a sketching pen, the column in the centre used a broad nibbed sketching pen and the column on the right employed a calligraphic pen. All the marks across the top of the columns are variations of line. Those across the middle represent tone and the marks at the bottom of each column show various types of texture. The tone, it will be seen, are basically combinations of line which obscure the paper to a greater or lesser extent. The textures are very similar to the tones but they employ dots, dashes, shapes and patterns and irregular line in order to suggest surface texture as well as tone. In practice, tone and texture may be interchangeable and the exact function of the marks depends on their context.

These illustrations show how the basic marks of pen and ink drawing may be expanded upon by using more than one pen or by employing additional techniques. Five of the examples show the use of two pens making similar marks, but in different sizes. The interaction between these creates the effect. The remaining four examples show the effects of drawing with a pen through thin tissue, drawing onto wet paper, alternately pulling and pushing the same pen and dabbing ink onto the paper off a crumpled tissue.

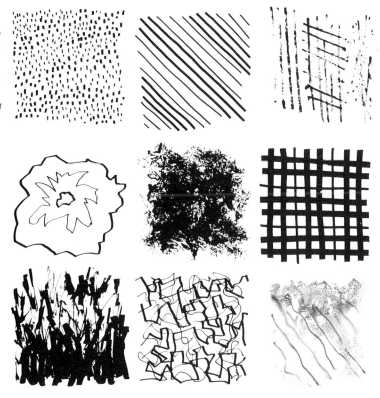

Control of the Pen

It is not enough to know what a pen can do if it cannot be made to do it whenever the artist wants. Control of the pen is the other essential ingredient that leads to successful pen and ink drawing. It can only be gained through accumulated experience, that means constant practise and experiment. It is possible though to make some general observations as to the behaviour of drawing pens that may shorten this process.

A pen is more easily pulled than pushed, so it always moves smoothly when moved toward the body. It may slide sideways on its tip in either direction, but again it works better if pulled. If a pen is moved forward, its angle to the paper should be lessened and the pressure on the nib should be reduced. The downward movement of the pen point produces a thick line, whilst a sideways movement produces a thin one. Increasing the pressure on the nib also thickens its mark. If this is undertaken within a pen stroke, a tapering line will result. The speed with which a pen is moved affects the mark it makes as well.

The pen should always rest comfortably in the hand and awkward movements of the hand or arm should be avoided. Instead the paper should be moved so that the desired mark can be made more easily. For essentially the same reasons, the long lines in pen drawings should be done in sections with the hand or the paper being moved between each.one. This prevents over-reaching which usually leads to a loss of control. Finally, note that all pens draw better once they have worn a little to suit the tilt of the artist's hand. Sketching pens should therefore be worked in with practise drawings until they begin to glide smoothly over the paper.

LINE

A simple line drawing on tinted ingres paper with white gouache used to create the pattern deriving from the striped jumper.

MALCOLM MACDONALD

This drawing of a potted
chrysanthemum was made by dipping
the pen from one pot of ink to another
to vary the colour. The drawing was
completed in outline and then broadly
filled in with a wash of the same inks.
To get the best out of coloured inks
your surface needs to be non-porous
e.g. Line board or paper, coated
printers' paper or a non bleed marker
pad.

Basic Line

Line can be incredibly suggestive if it is used skillfully, but it is difficult to master the use of line alone. It is even more difficult to minimise the use of line and to suggest the entire drawing with only a few strokes of the pen. In line drawing it is essential to concentrate on contours. Variety can be added and the lines may be made more suggestive by varying their thickness, or alternatively by contrasting lines of even but different thicknesses against each other.

Line and Solids

When line is used alone, a thickening of the line suggests shadow. This may be taken further by expanding the line into a solid area of darkness. By doing this where key shadows fall, a very positive sense of form can be created. A solid area of ink may also suggest a dark colour, not necessarily shadow and if it contains gaps to indicate highlights, it may also express form. Line contrasted against solids especially on white paper is economical yet effective and it may produce quite a forceful image.

This drawing makes use of two thick-nesses of even line. The composition creates a sense of distance and many c the lines lead the eye towards the sun.

This drawing was preplanned in pencil to make effective use of line and solid areas of ink. The highlights of the hair are reversed from the paper. In this part of the drawing, the solid represents colouring, but elsewhere it represents shadow. Note that a tiny amount of texture and tone has been added to set off the design, but essentially it remains a work in line and solids.

A very rapid drawing intended to capture the pose. Just a simple line made in non-waterproof ink which creates a pleasing diffusion when in contact with water as in this wash of watercolour.

A broad calligraphy nib was used to make this drawing. The colouring is achieved by dipping the pen between black ink, brown ink and water.

MALCOLM MACDONALD

TONE

This pen drawing employs tone in two
different ways. First of all it uses
hatching and cross hatching to create
areas of shadow and half-shadow, some
of this is done with a small calligraphy
pen which offers a choice between thick
and thin pen marks. A second tonal
element is introduced by the use of tinted
paper and two colours of ink. The initial
drawing is done in brown ink but parts of
it have been reworked over the top using
black ink. Further hatching in black over
the existing hatching in brown has
produced some subtle variations of
tone.

This study of leaves on a branch uses hatching and cross hatching to model the forms and to indicate shadow. The darker the shadow, the closer the hatching and the more it is crossed and recrossed. In places, the hatching is also used to indicate shape by curving it or by pointing it in a particular direction. Then to complete the effect, the tonal modelling of the subject matter has been emphasised by highlighting parts of the drawing with white pastel.

Hatching

The simplest way of introducing tone to a pen drawing is to hatch over parts of it. Hatching is the term given to parallel strokes of the pen which partly obscure the paper and make it look darker. If the hatching is repeated across the same area in a different direction, it is known as cross hatching and an even darker tonal value is created.

Highlighting

Hatching suppresses the brilliance of the paper and on a white background there is a limit to the subtlety that it can achieve. On tinted paper, the background already has a tonal value and hatching and cross hatching on top of that creates sub divisions of that tone. Softly tapering shadows are therefore easier to achieve. The lightest parts of the drawing however, will be comparatively dull and need to be brought forward by means of highlighting. That means going over parts of the coloured paper using white. White pastel or chalk is convenient to use, but white watercolour is also effective. Tonal drawings done in this manner can be quite beautiful.

Line and Wash

Where India ink is used for the drawing, tone may also be introduced by overlaying washes either of diluted ink or of watercolour. A single colour is used but it is diluted to different strengths so that it suppresses the brilliance of the paper to a greater or lesser extent. This creates additional tonal values which reinforce those already in the drawing.

Line and wash is closely related to watercolour painting and apart from being an attractive medium in its own right, it is ideally suited as a method of teaching or practising the art of watercolour. Line and wash requires good drawing and a disciplined use of tone. Both of these have advantages in painting also.

The illustrations on this page and the two that follow show a sequence of working in line and wash. The above illustration shows the initial pen drawing. A style has been chosen that suits the subject matter and in this case, a ruler has been used to make straight lines during inking in. The whole composition was carefully constructed in advance using a pencil. Note that tone is indicated in the drawing by stippling and very formal hatching. But only a limited amount of tone is added with the pen, the rest will be added with washes.

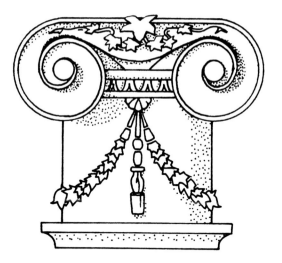

Following the layout of the pen drawing, thin flat washes have been applied to it to emphasise the existing tones and to create subtle intermediate tones. A decorative marble effect paper has been chosen as the background since it complements the subject matter of the drawing.

After the first washes have been allowed to dry, further stronger washes of the same colour have been applied. These provide the darkest tonal values and have also been used to add a little extra detail. Thinned India ink could have been used to tone this drawing, but a blue tint has been chosen instead to make the effect more lively.

'A Blasted Tree in a Landscape' c 1780 by Alexander Cozens. This sketch shows some of the rich textural effects that can be achieved using pen, ink and wash. Note how the foreground is accentuated with strong shadows whilst the background has been made to recede by using weaker tonal values, fine lines and pale washes.

TEXTURE

This illustration shows the beginning of
the drawing opposite. Two sizes of
calligraphy nib have been used in order
to make interesting marks from which
textural effects can be derived. The thin
outline of the background is achieved
by sliding a calligraphy nib sideways
across the paper. The basic idea is to
reduce the image of the landscape to a
mass of pattern. Details are not therefore
recorded accurately but are rendered
symbolically using bold strokes of the
pen.

MALCOLM MACDONALD

Gradually the whole drawing has been filled with texture. Note how some of the pen marks reflect the materials they record. Strong hard outlines around the stones for example and wavy wispy lines in the cloud. To avoid visual confusion, some of the areas of texture have been reinforced by a bold outline and here and there shadows have been strengthened.

Texture

Texture and tone are not the same thing, but in pen and ink drawing there are strong similarities between them. This is because textures also happen to represent tonal values because they suppress paper and for the sake of variety, textures and patterns are sometimes used to represent tone in place of hatching. The real difference is the intention behind the pen marks, not the marks themselves. Where textures are employed they are meant to be visually stimulating or they may be intended to convey a sense of the material they represent. Typical textural techniques include scribbling with a loosely held pen, stippling with the point of the nib or using squiggles or dashes in random groupings.

This drawing makes use of texture as well as tone and incorporates many different types of pen mark. Note that the use of hatching is also controlled so that it in effect it becomes a form of texture.

Pattern

Pattern incorporates texture, but it also embraces line and tone. Pattern is the bringing together of all these elements in order to convey the maximum possible amount of information. The use of pattern is not only concerned with a sequence of marks, it considers the size and shape of the space that they occupy and how they relate as a whole to other parts of the drawing.

This is the starting point for a drawing which uses texture and pattern to accurately portray the plumage of a bird. It started as a light pencil drawing which was then inked in as shown here. At this stage line has been employed to record the shape of the bird and to note the position of its wings and the large feathers around its tail. A dotted line has been used to make a few further indications of where feathers lie and some light textural shading has been started around the bird's head. Later on, the existing lines may be reinforced, but no more strong contours will be introduced and a pattern of textures and tones will be used to indicate any further shapes that are required.

As the drawing is filled in with a variety of textures and tones, an impression of the bird's plumage is being built up. At the same time, the form of the bird is being modelled. Since only one colour of ink is employed, the pen marks must be changed continually to indicate different colours in the plumage. These marks are also grouped in patterns to suggest different types of feather. Dotted lines are used to plan the work as it progresses as they are easily lost beneath the texturing.

This drawing of a Red-Breasted Merganser is now complete. In the final stages, a few areas were worked over again to harmonise the overall effect. Hatching, stippling, scribbling and textural marks of all kinds have been employed. If desired, this drawing which is in India ink could now be colourwashed with inks or watercolours to convert it into an accurate full colour study of the bird's plumage.

COLOUR

This pen painting of the sea was begun in the same manner as the illustration opposite. However, once the floods of ink had dried, work continued on it, using the same colours of ink and the same calligraphy pen. It has been drawn over several times. The chance formation of the wet pen drawing has been built upon and gradually a more refined and certain impression has been extracted. Obviously such drawings do not record accurately the scenes they represent, but they are inspired by them whilst giving free rein to the artist's imagination.

MALCOLM MACDONALD

his impressionistic sketch of the
ea shores has been undertaken using
oloured inks. The paper was first made
et with clean water and before it dried,
e ink was drawn into it. The pen was
en used to encourage the ink to flow in
ertain directions. Its track can still be
een as the metal nib has cut into the
oftened paper creating a network of
es where ink has collected. These add
subtle texture to certain parts of the
en painting and were intended, though
s not possible to control such effects
curately. With this technique, there is
danger of the pen damaging the paper
eriously if it is too wet, so whilst the pen
ay be used vigorously, it should not be
ed roughly.

Colour From Pens

Using coloured inks or, if dip pens are employed, using watercolours as well, any pen drawing technique can be modified to incorporate colour. There are lots of possibilities and very few limitations. In fact, if a brush is used in support of the pen, there are really no limitations at all, and pen drawing may become a kind of painting.

For sketching out of doors, a pen and a few well chosen inks are ideal. Rapid coloured drawings can be made faster than watercolour sketches. They may not offer the same subtlety of colour, but they can record a great amount of detail and can indicate colouring to a satisfactory degree for the purposes of a sketch. Alternatively, washes of ink or watercolour can be applied first, then pens and coloured inks can be used over the top. Coloured pen and ink drawings also combine well with pastel, especially if they are on tinted paper.

Colouring Drawings

A pen and ink drawing may anticipate the application of coloured washes from the outset or, if it has recorded the tones and textures of its subject properly, colour may be added later without disturbing the relationships within the drawing. Both these techniques are an extension of the principles of line and wash in which colour is used instead of shades of grey or some other neutral tone.

Preliminary drawings in dilute India ink make an excellent foundation for watercolour landscape paintings. However, coloured –over pen drawings are best suited to detailed subject matter where a finely executed drawing needs to dominate. Waterproof India ink should always be used for this purpose as the drawing will not be disturbed by the washes of colour. Pen drawings have the advantage over pencil here, of not being easily suppressed by the superimposed tints. All their detail, however fine, therefore remains visible.

This drawing of a wild orchid has been prepared for colouring in. It is detailed, but it is not fussy. Its use of tone is restrained and what hatching there is, is for the most part, widely spaced. This leaves plenty of paper free to give brilliance to the colour. Not all the pen lines record the detail exactly as it appears. The dotted lines around the edge of the leaves and the spots marked on the flowers show where colour changes occur and are a guide for the colouring process.

Pale washes of colour are put on to begin with. Large areas are filled in first with a well filled brush, but care is taken not to go over the outline or to overlap onto other areas of colour. Watercolours or dilute inks may be used, but watercolour paints are likely to offer greater permanence if they are wisely selected.

When the first washes have dried, stronger washes of colour are applied to indicate areas of shadow. These follow the areas of tone already indicated in the drawing. Any small areas of colouring that remain, like the edges of the leaves, are now filled in and to complete the painting a little extra detail is added with the brush.

"A Tile Factory" by Vincent Van Gogh.
Note the initial pencil sketch beneath
the ink. This rapid working gives a
vitality that could be lost by a more
painstaking and detailed approach.

FURTHER
EXAMPLES

These two pen drawings were carefully planned in pencil before being inked over, but much of the detail was invented and added whilst the pen was being used. Both drawings use a modified form of the line and solids style. In both cases, stippling has been added. This provides both tone and texture. Notice how stippling is used in some places to break the hard edge of an area of solid ink.

Straightforward hatching and cross hatching is evident on these two caricatures which imitate the style of a copperplate print. They began as loose pencil sketches showing nothing more than the stance and expressions. Their outlines were drawn first in pen and ink and the hatching was added afterwards, once the design of the figures was certain.

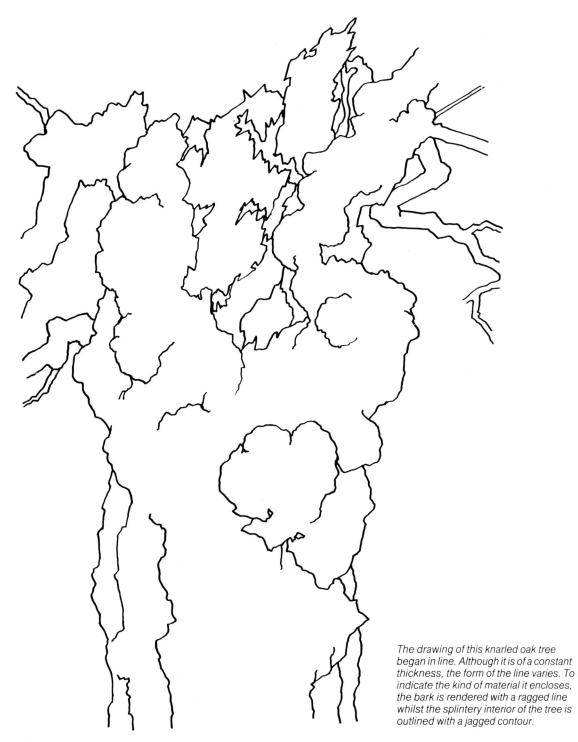

*The drawing of this knarled oak tree
began in line. Although it is of a constant
thickness, the form of the line varies. To
indicate the kind of material it encloses,
the bark is rendered with a ragged line
whilst the splintery interior of the tree is
outlined with a jagged contour.*

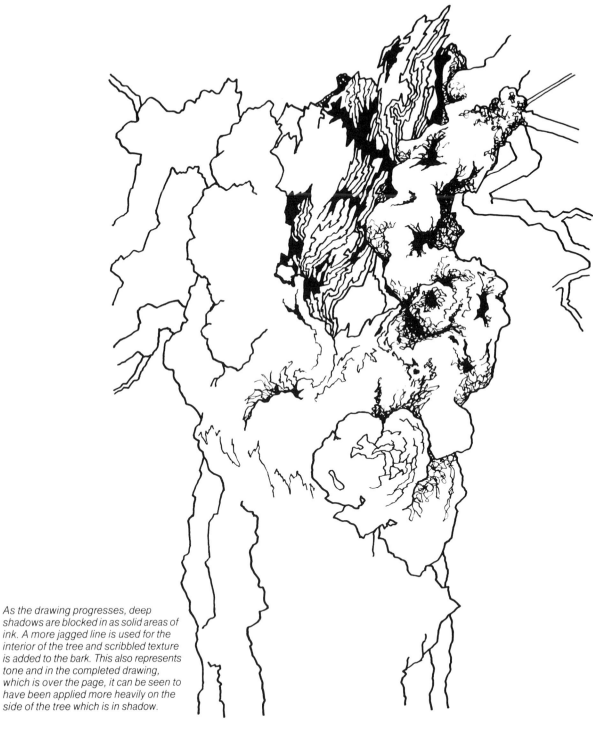

As the drawing progresses, deep shadows are blocked in as solid areas of ink. A more jagged line is used for the interior of the tree and scribbled texture is added to the bark. This also represents tone and in the completed drawing, which is over the page, it can be seen to have been applied more heavily on the side of the tree which is in shadow.

An uncluttered use of line is ideal in circumstances where a pen and ink drawing is intended to be attractive, yet has a technical purpose. This design for a jeweller's window display was actually constructed in pencil before pen and ink were used. The square frame which encloses the drawing was then inked in with the aid of a ruler but the rest of the drawing was gone over freehand. This keeps the style pleasantly informal, yet at the same time it is an accurate drawing.

These drawings of doorways were done with the aid of a ruler. The hatching and texture was applied freehand, but it is kept stiff and evenly spaced to reflect the solid character of the architecture. However, note how the line at the bottom of the door with the lion's head knocker is deliberately not straight to suggest a worn step. This small visual clue confirms what the style of the door already tells us, which is that it belongs to an old house.

These ideas for a decorative border are drawn with a bold sketching pen. They make use of strong line and solid areas of ink. They were planned in pencil to begin with and are designed around geometric shapes. The end pieces at the beginning of each chapter of this book were designed in the same way.

𝕿𝖍𝖊 𝕰𝖓𝖉

Osmiroid Creative Leisure Series

Each title in the Osmiroid Creative Leisure series has been written in a lively "to the point" style, with very practical advice to ensure that exciting creative results are quickly achievable.

Chinese Brush Painting includes Chinese Calligraphy and a host of ideas from animal and plant subjects to landscapes.

Colour Calligraphy explains colour theory and shows some of the many ways that imaginative colour calligraphy can be created.

chinese BRUSH PAINTING
by Pauline Cherrett

pen and ink DRAWING
by Jonathan Stephenson

colour CALLIGRAPHY
by Barbara Bundy

Osmiroid Creative Leisure Series

The Art of Sketching shows the reader how to approach sketching from a very practical viewpoint, covering a wide range of indoor and outdoor subjects.

The Art of Poster Making shows the reader how to create posters using the wide variety of media and ideas.

Art of Stencilling gives the reader all they need to know to stencil onto walls, fabrics, furniture or paper, with manufactured or home made stencils.

Design and artwork by Nigel Long, Winchester

Printed in Spain